# SUCCESSFUL JOB HUNTING

## The Smart Way

By

### Robert Lee Bauer

This book is a work of fiction. Places, events, and situations in this story are purely fictional. Any resemblance to actual persons, living or dead, is coincidental.

© 2002 by Robert Lee Bauer. All rights reserved.

No part of this book may be reproduced, stored in a retrieval system, or transmitted by any means, electronic, mechanical, photocopying, recording, or otherwise, without written permission from the author.

ISBN: 1-4033-3266-5 (E-book)
ISBN: 1-4033-3267-3 (Paperback)
ISBN: 1-4033-3268-1 (Dustjacket)

Library of Congress Control Number: 2002092089

This book is printed on acid free paper.

Printed in the United States of America
Bloomington, IN

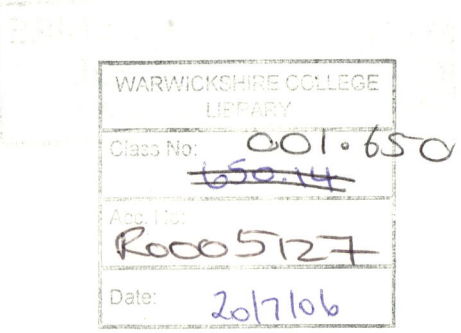

1st Books - rev. 07/26/02

## Notice to readers:

The rules, laws, advice, recommendations, guidance and other information contained herein constitute the opinions, experiences and education of the author of this book alone, and are in no situation meant to go against established laws, legal bindings, company procedures of any firm or group or other establishments in any way whatsoever. All contracts signed by prospective employers, employees, agencies, their representatives, unions and groups, are to be adhered to, as per all laws and rules governing each instrument and agreement. All individuals entering into agreements and bindings are responsible for their own actions and obligations.

# Table of Contents

Introduction ................................................................. vii
  I. PREPARATION ................................................... 3
     GOALS ............................................................. 3
     INVENTORY ................................................. 24
     PLANS ............................................................ 33

  II. SEARCHING ....................................................... 44
     RESUME ........................................................ 44
     COVER LETTER ........................................... 52
     NINE RESUME LAWS ................................. 54
     ADS ................................................................ 61
     APPLICATIONS ............................................ 68
     AGENCIES .................................................... 72
     STATE OFFICES .......................................... 79

  III. INTERVIEWING ................................................ 84
     PREPARATION ............................................. 84
     TWENTY-ONE INTERVIEW LAWS ........... 87
     POST INTERVIEW ....................................... 90

  IV. ACCEPTING ...................................................... 97
     CONFIRMATION .......................................... 97
     REVIEW ........................................................ 99
     ACCEPTANCE ............................................ 100
     SUMMARY .................................................. 101
     LIST OF ITEMS .......................................... 103

# Introduction

# Introduction

The most successful executives will follow the most elementary routes when they are means to occupationally beneficial ends: high-paying jobs.

If you are serious about getting a good position without wasting time, money, and gasoline, then consider the information contained herein and prepare to become a salesman with a very important product: you.

You have to develop a brochure (resume), sales technique, plan of attack, set of contacts, procedures, follow-up and the close of the sale strategy.

Included are a list of resume laws and a list of interview laws to follow. Whether you are an executive who was making $175,000 per year or an hourly worker used to making minimum wage, you will benefit by the information contained herein. Each phase of this operation, "Finding That Perfect Job" is equally as important as the next, and cannot stand alone. If you have a perfect resume, interview perfectly, know exactly where you stand, and leave the employer no phone number or address with which to contact you, all is lost. None of these phases is simple by itself. They only become simple when done in proper sequence and done thoroughly.

Politicians running for office always hire a sales person or team to make them look good on television. One simply does not go out and "do her best" to be elected anymore. That is not enough. We have learned that the pursuit of a job is a task for the "sales" type of people to instruct us. There is a bit of psychology, a bit of organization and a lot of salesmanship. This may sound a bit off the track of what you think job searching should be, but the biggest, most important sale of your life is the one of selling yourself to your, hopefully, new boss.

Naturally, there will not be extra credits on your college transcript that you did not earn, but we need to make every bit of experience and education, as well as the host of assets you innately possess, all come together in an attractive presentation that will make the employer want you more than any other applicant.

If any one paragraph helps you obtain a more lucrative or more satisfying position with a company, then this book is well worth reading. A wise person will consider all that is suggested before closing her mind and deciding on a course of action.

Many successful professionals have never had to prepare a resume and never had an urge to leave the position they were in and, consequently, are 100% new to the present day job-search task. Relax. You may obtain all of the information you need in every area. Whether you are an old hand at job searching or a newcomer, there are many talented and currently informed professionals at hand for each task involved. There are employment agencies to help present you to companies looking for your type, there are resume writers to enlighten you on the fine art of creating your sales brochure on yourself, and state offices to find jobs, without charge. Each company is different, and job hunting techniques change commensurately. All you really need is this book, a pen and paper.

There are far more resources available today to the unemployed person than ever before in history. The ambitious person will take advantage of every opportunity and check them thoroughly. Good luck.

*Successful Job Hunting*

# Preparation

*Robert Lee Bauer*
# Goals

# Inventories

# Plans

# CHAPTER I
# PREPARATION

## GOALS

Successful job searching can yield a lifetime of benefits both emotionally and monetarily. It is like a roller coaster ride with chills and thrills. One minute you may be elated, and the next minute depressed. It affects your life and your future. The main objective of this book is to condition you to be a salesman and get precisely the position you want. It can be fun. We want to guarantee success as best we can. Let's swing the chances our way. We need to eliminate as many of the negative surprises as we can. The goal is to increase the odds extremely into your favor for finding that choice job. You need to first define your personal vision of "choice job." Here are the steps toward doing just that.

There are many things you need to do first in preparation for achieving that goal. Setting the goals is one of them.

- What are goals?

- Why do we have them?

- Does everyone have goals?

- How often do they change?

- Do I have to have them?

- What can setting goals do for me?

- Why have short-term goals?

Goals are our <u>reasons</u> for living! (Consciously or subconsciously.) Everyone alive has both short-term and long-term goals.

Why not decide what goals we want, and live toward them? Write them down. Tell everyone about them. Our goals change as we change in physical and mental makeup, and as our needs change through life. We need to constantly revise our goals to our latest needs and wants. They need to be set with two guiding factors considered. We need to establish goals that are high enough to make us extend ourselves fully in life, but close enough to be reached by taking small steps. We are more solidly established at our various levels when we have reached them by taking small steps. Heights achieved via leaps and bounds are not firm and well established. For example, the person who wins a ten-million-dollar lottery is not accustomed to the habits and practices of the reliable investing of typical multimillionaires, and may lose it all rapidly. Such extremes are hard on our emotions and our nerves. Rapid changes are seldom beneficial.

Our bodies and our minds actually change slowly. The goals that we set for ourselves need to reflect and accommodate this characteristic commensurately. The higher the goal (from where we are now) the further away, in time, it should be set. Our super-high-set goals being placed too near put too much pressure on us and allows for few mistakes. We humans are regularly and innately erring as we go through life, even when we try to be cautious.

Short-term goals need to be established to provide incentive, accomplishment, reassurance, and confidence as we proceed toward our ultimate goals. Don't restrict your goals to financial and materialistic types of listings. We simply mention goals and right away people think of amounts of money they can build for retirement, types of houses they want, and types of cars they want. Establish goals for yourself that will allow and cause you to extend yourself emotionally and mentally. Everyone thinks that goals are nice and we should set them for ourselves. Actually, goals are more than simply nice. They are necessities, and extremely essential in life. They guide us and control us. They give us purpose, excitement, happiness, contentment, achievement, pleasure, fulfillment, cause, drive, energy and enthusiasm. Goals are life's reasons and directions. Let's set them intentionally, rather then simply waiting to see what life deals us at random.

The main reason for establishing goals for ourselves is to create two essential drives that we vitally require for happiness: energy and enthusiasm.

Both short-term goals and long-term goals "create" energy and enthusiasm in us. Create endless energy and enthusiasm in yourself – set firm goals in your life and live toward them. The energy and enthusiasm will fuel your happiness fire for the rest of your life. There is no end to it. In fact, it grows stronger and stronger with each little accomplishment and each little step toward your goals. Learn your true likes, desires and needs in life. Learn the tremendous satisfaction gained in helping others in some small way. It gives life a zest that is unmatched in any way. There are three "major" life goals that all of us need to use along with our individual goals:

1. "Accept" life as it comes, and everyone in it.

2. "I make myself rich by making my wants fewer," as stated by Thoreau. See how "little" you can get by with instead of how much.

3. "Release" happiness and feelings, good or bad. Never stew or simmer for more than a <u>minute</u>. Let out the laughs and the smiles. Open up. Let out the opinions and displeasures as they come. Be honest.

There are also two "minor" goals that everyone needs to add into the list of individual goals:

1. The "three" things needed to succeed at anything are: hours, hours, hours. Whether it be a job, art, piano, or sports perfection, you need to put in hours, hours, hours on it, to succeed.

2. The "three" things needed to succeed at any type of social interfacing, relationship, or partnership are: listen, listen, listen.

Major Goals:

1. "Accept" life and people.

2. Have "fewer wants."

3. "Release" happiness and displeasure.


Minor Goals:

1. We need "hours, hours, hours."

2. We need to "listen, listen, listen."

*Robert Lee Bauer*

Put the following words into your goals that you design just for you. Sprinkle them around.

| | |
|---|---|
| Cheerfulness | Gladness |
| Goodness | Joyfulness |
| Enjoyment | Fascination |
| Captivation | Blissfulness |
| Delight | Sunshine |
| Contentment | Enchantment |
| Peace | Serenity |
| Gratification | Merriment |
| Pleasure | Exhilaration |
| Enthusiasm | Graciousness |
| Devotion | Loving |
| Smiling | Happy |

Also, you might want to throw in a few minor goal words such as these:

| | |
|---|---|
| Lucky | Fortunate |
| Thrilled | Elevated |
| Jolly | Laughing |
| Heavenly | Carefree |

When making goals, think of what you really like and want. Think of what makes you the happiest. When did you really enjoy life the most? What are the things that really make you feel good about yourself?

What would you do with your time if you had a million dollars and did not have to work? Would you make a goal of going back to school, or taking a course, or learning something new?

Points in establishing goals:

- Make both short-term goals and long-term goals.
- Write them on paper.
- Tell your goals to everyone.

- Read them daily and adjust them to your life's needs as it progressively changes.

- Keep them realistic, but aim high because you are probably a lot more talented than you think you are.

- Realize that your whole life is governed by goals. Establish your own.

- Remember: the things you think about most become your life, so make them the most desirable goals by planning them with careful consideration.

Decide what types of jobs you would enjoy doing. For example, check one in each of the following categories:

- Working indoors or working outdoors?
- Working with a product, working with people, or working with a service?
- Working with health care, entertainment, merchandise, transportation, real estate, other?
- Do you like to sell, read, draw, manage, analyze, drive, care for, teach, travel, write, entertain, build, photograph, model, other?

Points About Employment:

- Learn what you really like.

- Pursue it thoroughly.

- Go all-out for it.

- Don't settle for less.

- Make it a goal for yourself and work hard toward achieving it, in being able to say, "I am really happy with my job." You deserve it and you owe it to yourself. <u>It is your choice</u>.

*Robert Lee Bauer*

Goals Checklists:

Short-term (3 – 5 years) Goals:

1. _____

   _____

   _____

2. _____

   _____

   _____

3. _____

   _____

   _____

4. _____

   _____

   _____

Note: Include occupational, financial, physical, religious, personal, etc.

*Robert Lee Bauer*

Long-term (3 – 5 years) Goals:

1. _____

   _____

   _____

2. _____

   _____

   _____

3. _____

   _____

   _____

4. _____

   _____

   _____

*Successful Job Hunting*

Note: Include occupational, financial, physical, religious, personal, etc.

*Robert Lee Bauer*
## INVENTORY

The inventory consists of several lists. We need to make a list of: emotions, education, finances, experience, and various other factors.

- List all funds and access to various funds (i.e., savings, emergency monies, etc.).

- List all budgets, charts and payment schedules that need attention while you are unemployed.

- Consider calling all creditors for a moratorium from payments or to make interest-only payments until you are gainfully employed. Make small token payments, but be sure to include a letter with each payment to explain why it is not

*Successful Job Hunting*

the normal amount. This shows good faith on your part. A very small amount monthly is far better than skipping a payment completely. Telling them "why" is even more important.

- Attempt to refinance or to consolidate loans to make ends meet.

- If you are heavily involved financially, and you cannot meet your obligation, you should consider seeing a county finance counselor to handle your payments. He will give you an allowance out of your funds and pay small payments from any assets. He can also counsel you on which way to go and how to obtain county assistance. This service is usually free, if unemployed.

- Summarize all assets and all liabilities to know exactly where you stand. Add up all outstanding bills, and then add up all values of material items plus any cash, bonds, savings, stocks, valuables, etc. Subtract the totals and that is your net worth. Learn just exactly how much you will need to get by for the next few months while job searching. Find out how much you are eligible for as far as unemployment goes, part-time jobs, other incomes, etc.

- List all insurances and their respective payments and grace periods, benefits, possible amounts, etc.

- Check mortgage payments, benefits, grace periods, equity loans available, and the possibilities of refinancing with a different loan company. A new mortgage loan with a lower percentage rate could possible have a lower payment per month.

- List all part-time and temporary work agencies and centers including state-run centers, as well as where to go for free services, employment information, assistance, and money. County medical services are usually free if you are without income. List all phone numbers and addresses you can find.

There are unemployment workshops for group counseling in many areas of the larger cities. Many people have a problem with emotional depression from unemployment. Being out of work, losing personal possessions, being turned down when applying for work, and many other aspects of this situation can lead to a serious depression with some people. Depression is not to be let go unchecked as it can snowball rapidly. Get with friends and family and talk about everything that bothers you. Get it all out on the table. Discuss it with others. Do not keep it all to yourself. Sharing some of your worry lessens it to a great extent. Seek counseling from a free clinic if possible. Realize that you are not a salesperson and not used to the rejections that normally accompany job searching. Open up to everyone and anyone. Let go of all hatreds and resentments, as well as any regrets. They are all anchors pulling you down mentally. Be responsible and let out all that anger turned inward. Do what you really want to do, and do it the way you want. Be yourself.

Review all inventories, lists, charts, tasks, schedules, and start your new life as a whole new person. Think <u>positive</u> and think <u>happy</u>. Happiness is not what happens to us in life, it is how we let our minds think happy. Let go right this very minute

*Robert Lee Bauer*
with a big smile. You deserve it. Be happy by letting

yourself be happy.

Review each of these items:

- Inventory of bills:

- Inventory of funds:

- Lists of jobs to do while looking for full-time jobs:

- Lists of addresses of part-time/temporary work centers:

- Unemployment offices to visit:

- Chamber of Commerce books picked up:

- Private employment agencies to visit:

- Yellow Pages and other phone books to check:

- Newspapers to subscribe to and check:

- Magazines to buy to check trade jobs:

- Library books to consult/check-out (on salaries, jobs, fields, resumes, benefits):

- County agencies/centers to check all that is available in the way of medical, employment, unemployment, finances, counseling, courses, pamphlets, classes, computers, benefits, forms, application, open jobs, and all possible help:

- Computer websites to check (i.e., www.dol.gov for the Department of Labor information):

## PLANS

Happiness with a new job requires diligent planning, searching and interviewing. Prior to the searching and interviewing is the extremely important phase of knowing exactly where you stand at present, and where you want to go. Then comes the planning for getting there.

Knowing where you stand is a matter of taking inventory. Job searching is a sales function. One has to learn to accept the odds of failure and success of sales. A great many places may be contacted before being hired. It has nothing to do (necessarily) with your talents if there are no openings. Naturally, your talents will have a great bearing on your securing a position if there is one. It may be difficult to find an opening right off. Many professionals are used to seeing success and results in their daily jobs, and find it very difficult to accept a sales result of 2% to 5% success. This is not to say that all professional individuals see 100 companies before landing a job. One may find a job at the first one visited, but that would not be the average case.

Be prepared to accept in stride the various disappointments that come along with normal job searching. Establish a plan and follow it. Determine the type of job, quantity of resumes, areas of interest, and all the particulars for your written plan. Once the plan is on paper, you can revise it as necessary or follow it to the letter. To find an eight-hour-a-day job, one should spend <u>eight hours a day</u>

*Successful Job Hunting*

<u>looking for that job</u>. Planning for job searching includes bringing our perspective into focus.

Concentrate on your true desires. List them all on a piece of paper. List every single item as you think of it; then go back over your list to make sure you have everything you want.

When you have all of your desires listed, imagine yourself as already having them. Imagine that your life has been that way for the last couple of years, and you are used to it. What new goals and desires would you list? Where do you go from here? Will this be enjoyable forever, or are there further needs? If all of your dreams came true this very minute, what would be your driving force to keep you enthusiastic and looking forward? Are all of those items actually needed to make you happy?

If most of your goals and desires are material items, then your perspective may not be on target. If any of the items are dependent on the actions of others, then you need to review your attitude and feelings. We need to realize that we can only control ourselves; and that it's far better that way, or life would lose its sparkle and spontaneity of individualism. The intricate complexities of uniqueness would fall away to boredom and total predictability. Some people give us great joy, and there are some who give us heartburn. Those are just the tears and cheers of life, without which we could not enjoy it to its fullest.

Your perspective on happiness needs to be aimed at the reason why you are not totally and thoroughly happy now, and how you can make that situation a temporary one. Find a job.

Our perspective of placing importance on the things in our lives takes on a different light when we learn what others are going through. Why wait for something super wonderful, or a tragedy, to make us learn what is important to us. In other words, if we know and we have seen what makes us feel good, then why don't we impose those feelings on ourselves without the actual stimulus happening?

If you have only two years to live, see if you can cheer someone's life who only has six months to live. He will definitely appreciate the caring from someone like you.

The broadest smile that I've seen in years was that of a lady who had sold a painting she had just finished. It was a goal, an achievement, an income, a delight, and a task done in perspective. She was extremely happy, as she had painted the picture by holding the brushes in her teeth. She has no arms.

The most important page you could ever read, as shown in "Human Development Across the Life Span" by Hughes and Noppe (1985) … "Abraham Maslow, trained in behaviorist psychology, suggested that man has five basic needs: physiological, safety and security, need for belongingness and love, self-esteem, and self-actualization needs. Self-actualization being the need to fulfill their unique potential."

*Robert Lee Bauer*

Qualities of self-actualization:

- Accurate perception of reality
- Acceptance of self and others
- Spontaneous and natural behaviors
- Concern with problems rather than self
- Need for privacy and detachment
- Independence of judgment
- Continuous freshness of appreciation
- Mystic or peak experiences
- Desire to help improve humanity
- Few, but deep, friendships
- Genuine belief in democratic values
- Strong sense of right and wrong
- Philosophical, not hostile, humor

- Interest in novelty and creativity

- Resistance to cultural conventions

*Robert Lee Bauer*

Points of Perspective:

- Understanding

- Self-accepted

- Realistic

- Optimistic

- Moderate

- Giving

- Decision maker

Thoreau: "I make myself rich by making my wants fewer."

*Successful Job Hunting*

# Searching

# CHAPTER II
# SEARCHING

## RESUME

A resume is simply a "brochure" to entice the employer to ask you to come in to talk. Let it remain that way. The more you write, the more he has with which to eliminate you from the possibility of an interview. If someone mailed you a brochure of a vacuum cleaner and had 15 pages of capabilities, how many of those pages would you read? Would you consider tossing it in the basket? A one-page resume these days for busy bosses is almost a must. Also, a color snapshot in a shoulder-up business pose is another selling point that used to be unheard of, but is now very beneficial.

Have you ever heard of an employer simply saying, "Yes, I like his resume, so call him with a salary offer, and state the day that he's to start"? I can't imagine that you've heard that very often. Generally, an employer would like to see the applicants and talk to them in person before they hire them. In fact, employers all over the country are sending airline tickets to possible employees simply to have them come over to talk about a position that has been written about in reams of paper already. Why not let him see you at the outset, along with your brochure of past accomplishments? Again, list on your resume only the pertinent facts and attractions that are eye openers to a reader, and only recent (five to 10 years) of history. We want him to ask to see you. Never list a single item that you have not done (naturally), as you may be called upon to prove it. Be honest, sincere, open, but most of all, factual and realistic. Keep in mind very strongly the goal of what you want to do. Do not limit yourself. You can probably perform a great deal more than you realize. Most people underestimate their abilities and find out that it is really a small world and, when thoroughly familiarized with a given task, they can perform it with ease, regardless of a lofty title.

Follow the enclosed nine resume laws to the letter, and draw up a rough copy. Type or print the rough copy and, if need be, take it to a resume writer. There are some listed in your phone book, and some listed on the Internet. The choice is yours.

After you read this paragraph, follow the laws, see the examples, check the library resume books and the computer offerings, then you are ready. You don't have a cobbler work on your transmission, and you don't have a mechanic work on your shoes. Every resume book in the library can probably give you some ideas, but they are dated, as is this book. You may need a current professional to give you the best results.

Do not play games with your future. You may be saying that you are certainly capable of writing a paper on yourself because you wrote a thesis for your Ph.D., but unless it was on salesmanship or advertising, you should bend your pride a little and see the specialist. Never mention salaries, sicknesses, restrictions of any kind, ages, or birth dates unless, for some strange reason, they are to your benefit. For all practical purposes, they will more likely hinder than help.

Keep the resume limited to simply getting an interview, and the other facts and technical abilities can emerge at that time. Don't let the resume start toward getting you the position and how well you could do it. Do mention things such as being married and long tenures, whether they are in living in one place or being at one job a long time. Tenure on any point is stability to an employer, and that is a major asset in his eyes. Always mention schools and courses of any type whatsoever. Any learning that you have obtained, even for a hobby, can be a plus for you in his eyes. The small color snapshot can be made at a local photographer (in bulk) cheaper than you could do it yourself, in most cases.

After the resume writer returns your finished copy, you can take it to the printer and have your 200 copies printed on the offset. You may use a heavier paper, such as 50- or 70-pound paper, as it is more sophisticated looking and much more impressive to the future boss reading it. Colored paper is a must for sales. Equally as important as color is the lighter shade. If a dark shade of color is used, it is too hard to read. A pastel or light beige, shades of brown, or very light yellow are attractive and easy to read. Don't be flashy. (A boss with three resumes will remember the one with the photo.)

Now that you have a definite goal, a finance chart, 200 resumes, 200 color photos and some envelopes, you are ready to start. The Chamber of Commerce offices can sell you an industrial guide that lists manufacturers, service agencies, etc., by company size, address, etc. Some Chambers show these on their websites.

You should also keep everyone in the neighborhood supplied with your resume copies (unless you desire to keep your search a secret). A neighbor can give a resume to a friend's friend who might just come up with your choice slot in life.

*Successful Job Hunting*

Also, see that relatives, friends, groups, organizations, and societies are informed of your desires. Why turn down help?

*Robert Lee Bauer*
## COVER LETTER

When sending a resume to a prospective employer for an interview, always send it under a cover letter introducing yourself. Explain that you want an interview, and ask them to consider your enclosed resume for any openings in the near future. Always include phone numbers and your email address.

*Successful Job Hunting*

# Resume Laws

*Robert Lee Bauer*
## NINE RESUME LAWS

1. Easy reading and proper spacing (double spacing preferred).

2. Job objective first, after name, address, and telephone, plus a message number.

3. Only complimentary, fitting words, of simple nature.

4. Simple, fast reading facts with no superfluous organizational terms. Use verbs under each job listing (i.e., created, wrote, developed, supervised).

5. No job dates, simply years on each job if over a year, unless four or less jobs. Never cover more than the last 10 years of experience, or last three jobs.

6. Only pertinent, advantageous, personal information.

7. Keep your resume as an introduction and let the interview do the detailing. The more you write, the more they have with which to eliminate you, without an interview.

8. Always write a cover letter introducing yourself, and a brief description, stating in which department you would like to work.

9. Be sure to enclose the small photo and card with telephone numbers.

(See "sample resume" on next page.)

*Robert Lee Bauer*

# Resume

William Lee Barnes, Jr.  B.S.E.E. – Missouri University
1234 Lynn Drive  12 hrs. toward M.B.A. – USC
Callora, CA 91737  Corres. Courses – Mgt. & Supv.
Home:   415-322-0908  Member – A.S.Q.C.
Message: 415-322-6757  Service: U.S.A.F. – Lieutenant
         (Neighbor)

Objective:   Quality Engineering Supervision or Quality Auditing

Personal:    Enjoy working with people, conscientious, creative, capable of high volume, published two technical research analyses on micro hybrid I.C. failure analyses, staff writer on ASQC.

Martell-Cablette    Quality engineer, product reliability
(five years)        trending, technical writing, test analyses. Created procedures and designed tests.

Adams Corporation   Engineering planner and scheduler,
(three years)       drawing checker, liaison analyses engineer, R&D development responsibility. Approved drawings, created guidelines.

Brooks Research     Electronic supervisor in production,
(two years)         product planning, cost analyses, personnel (24) supervisor with hire and fire responsibilities. Reported progress. Created assembly drawings and guidelines.

References furnished upon request.

Mail your resumes to every possible contact regardless of whether or not you know if positions are available. Sometimes a position may be in the creating phase and you could miss out by simply saying to yourself that you are sure that this particular company has no need of your services. You may have heard that they definitely do not need a person in your field today and, all of a sudden, the boss says that he does need someone like you.

In other words, don't shut any doors on yourself; there will be enough of them shut on you as it is. Don't be discouraged because the sales field is a different breed of business than what you are probably used to dealing with. An engineer may develop five designs and only have to revise one of them a small amount before going into production, whereas, a salesman might see 100 people before he chalks up three sales.

Your odds are most likely going to be a bit different from what you're used to seeing. That's why many people get discouraged while job hunting. They simply are not used to sales results. If you get two interviews out of 60 resumes, you may think you have something wrong with you, and a salesman might say that he wishes he had that kind of good luck. Keep your thoughts in perspective to realistic results and fight-on confidently. The stakes are annual salaries, and the product is your future.

Items to consider:

- Type of job seeking:

- Location preference:

- Limits of travel:

- Salary range:

- Objectives:

- Quantity of resumes:

- Quantity of photos:

- Quantity of contacts:

- Type of cover letter needed:

- Addresses and phone numbers:

- References to be listed:

- Transportation needed:

- Budget needed while job searching:

*Robert Lee Bauer*

# ADS

## ADS

Check the ads on the types of websites such as: http://CareerBuilders.com, http://jobsearching.org, http://JobHuntersBible.com, and http://www.dol.gov.

Resumes being mailed to 100 or 200 companies listed in the Chamber of Commerce book of businesses is only scratching the surface in "Job Searching" work. There are many links to websites that can help you find work. Check the Yellow Pages, also.

All ads need to be scanned and tried. Never discount a job until you have talked with the person needing to hire someone. Ads are always misleading, to some degree, from what the employer is actually looking for. Answer them all. You can always turn down a job if you so desire. Send a cover letter and a resume, or go visit them in person and speed up the process.

Check all newspapers, magazines, trade journals, bulletin boards, neighbors, friends, etc. Ads sometimes need to be interpreted, especially the qualifications you will need and the description of the job. They invariably ask for the moon in an ad, when someone without any of those credentials might very well be capable of performing the task. Toss your hat in the ring and try for the position you want in life.

The job descriptions often state that you will run everything and everyone when, in all reality, you may do quite another list of tasks. Don't forget their ad is like your resume in that it is a "grabber" to be appealing enough to lure top talent at the bottom price. Go check it out. Don't discard any possibilities. Try to remain optimistic and enthusiastic during the whole process.

Just go apply and see for yourself what is really needed.

Enter an ad in the "Jobs Wanted" column.

*Robert Lee Bauer*

Resume Copies Sent to Companies:

Name _____

Company _____

Address _____

Telephone _____


Name _____

Company _____

Address _____

Telephone _____


Name _____

Company _____

Address _____

*Successful Job Hunting*

Telephone _____


Name _____

Company _____

Address _____

Telephone _____


Name _____

Company _____

Address _____

Telephone _____


Website _____


Website _____

*Robert Lee Bauer*

    Website  _____


    Website  _____

*Successful Job Hunting*

# Applications

## APPLICATIONS

Brighten your day by taking a completed application along with you every day. Applications are the dirty work of Job Searching. No one likes to complete them or even ask someone to do one. Everyone has to do them to get a job though. Take a copy of one along with you when you apply in person at each new business. Even if it is on a different format or from a different company, the dates, salaries, names, addresses, and phone numbers are all the same for you. Copying them off of another sheet is three-times faster and more comfortable than creating them anew each time.

Some people take an hour and a half completing a twenty-minute application, then drive across town and do it all over again. Ask for a photocopy of your first one completed. They will be happy to make a copy for you. You deserve a copy of any item you apply your signature to, anyway. You are taking a pledge with binding verbiage and need to keep one copy for yourself. You don't need to tell them it is just to copy onto the next company's application.

Inquire as to the possibility of your stapling your resume to the application in lieu of completing the "Job History" portion of the application. Some firms will allow this, some will not.

Many firms now have attachments that state "optional" on the top of the sheet attached to the application. You are not required by law to complete them. They contain personal information such as sex, age, etc. It helps the company, state, and federal organizations when you do complete them, though, and it is not information that you would not relate to someone freely. It helps the company with statistics and many other reasons when you fill out the optional portions of applications.

Always attach a resume and a photo, if possible, to each application. Enter as many phone numbers as you possibly can. It would be terrible if your choice job were lost because they could not contact you about their decision. It happens every day.

*Successful Job Hunting*

# Visit the Agencies

## AGENCIES

Now that you have a definite goal, a finance chart, 200 resumes, 200 cover letters, envelopes, a set of contacts, people all over looking for jobs for you, resumes covering all the boss' desks in the county, and a calm confident head on your shoulders, the place you should go next is to every professional agency that you have listed in the phone book.

An employment agency counselor can paint a picture for you of the existing market for your product – you. He can tell you what your services are worth on the open market and if your idea of what they are worth is within the parameters of present reality or not. Never pay a fee, though (unless it is a special situation – usually companies pay the fees.) This counselor can be worth his weight in gold to you if you use him correctly. That is, be absolutely open, honest, blunt, and thorough within the limits of the task that you are seeking to perform occupationally. You don't have to hold back any secrets from him in any way, shape, or form. Unlike the interview laws, you can argue or whatever you like. The more you say and do, the more he'll learn what kind of a person you are.

A good counselor can probably tell you more about what your profession is earning than you can, and she can pile up all of your points such as education, experience, personal, etc., and come up with a fast, accurate figure for your potential annual value. Always give your professional agency counselor a complete run-down of your activities and whereabouts. Her newly found opening or interview is not worth a dime to you if she can't locate you. Keep her informed daily and, in active days, hourly, with respect to a phone number for you.

Now, if one counselor can do all that for you, why not multiply your chances by seeing many more counselors at other agencies. Some professionals have fallen into a rut of staying with one counselor after the first visit because he was nice and fair to him. Would you visit a counselor that was gruff, honest, loud, and got you four thousand a year more in wages?

An agency may be more than capable of finding an opening through contacts and, yet, not have a particular opening listed on the books. Many applicants have gone into an office and said, "I'm an engineer or chemist, do you have an opening?" An hourly worker who paints ball bat tips looks in the newspaper for ball bat painters. A professional seeking a professional slot fitting him to the tee sees a counselor that guides him into that slot and works with him every inch of the way. Again, you may be new to the sales field even if you have 25 years of executive experience in your field.

See the up-to-date professional in the task you're undertaking at present. Call all of them at the intervals that they recommend you call. Don't continue to call them regarding their results on your behalf, though. For example, if you are an attorney and you've gone to an agency that specializes in C.P.A.'s and accountants, you might only have a slim chance of hearing of their success in your behalf. Most generally, a specialist will let you know at the outset of his intentions in aiding your search or not. Don't be afraid to ask them to try for you, though. They may have many more contacts than you do and can easily get word to the person with whom you would like an interview.

The more open and honest and thorough you are with a counselor, the more you enable him or her to reciprocate with initiative in your behalf. If you tell him nothing and never call him, his efforts will probably be commensurate. Remember, never pay a fee (unless it is a special situation). Tell the counselor, and write it across the top of their application, that you "will never pay a fee for a job." Why not be offered many situations and be able to select the one that you want, as opposed to closing all of the doors except the only one perfect situation? Keep the odds high in your favor. The agency work should only be 5% of your interviewing. The bulk of the searching should be on your own. Don't forget, to obtain a 40-hour-per-week job you need to spend 40 hours per week looking for one.

Visit the firms listed in the Chamber of Commerce book of businesses, along with the

Yellow Pages, and submit an application, resume, and photo every place you would like to work. Don't wait for ads or agencies; go for it on your own. You will do just great.

## STATE OFFICES

Check your phone books for all state and local employment, unemployment, human resources, job finders, benefits offices, etc.

The library computers or your personal computer can show you such items as Jobs/Wages/Employers/Job Searching/etc.

The Department of Labor website is www.dol.gov.

*Robert Lee Bauer*

Searching Checklist:

Resumes created by: _____

_____

Resumes copies at: _____

_____

Photos at: _____

_____

Cover letters copied at: _____

_____

Agencies to see: _____

_____

_____

_____

State Offices to see: _____

*Successful Job Hunting*

Magazines/Trade Journals to buy: _____

_____

_____

Newspapers to buy: _____

_____

Computer ads to answer: _____

_____

_____

_____

Friends, neighbors, relatives to give/send resume copies to:

*Robert Lee Bauer*

*Successful Job Hunting*

# Interviewing

# CHAPTER III
# INTERVIEWING

PREPARATION

List all items that you wish to take with you on each interview. Gather all applicable work samples, resumes, photos, sample of completed application, and notes for the interview.

List all questions you need to ask: salary, tasks, hours, benefits, promotions, insurances. Have a sample of your work to present as evidence of your experiences, if possible. Take at least two resumes and two photos to leave in Personnel and with the possible future boss.

Prepare to ask for the job if you really want it. Know ahead of time what absolute minimum wage you can accept. Ask if the job is part time, temporary, full time, seasonal, consultant, contract, etc. Leave no surprises for yourself.

Take phone numbers and letters of recommendation, along with references' addresses and phone numbers.

*Robert Lee Bauer*
# Interview Laws

## TWENTY-ONE INTERVIEW LAWS

1. Appearance is very important. Dress for the job as a worker, not a slob nor a showman.
2. Be prepared and allow time.
3. Be alert, cheerful and ambitions, and have good posture.
4. Have information about their company, if you can.
5. Know something of their division, if you can.
6. Know something of the job involved, if you can.
7. Shake hands firmly.
8. Always arrive on time and alone.

9. Let the interviewer control the sequence of subjects.

10. Do not lie.

11. Never criticize former employers or fellow employees. (The way you speak of past employers is how they will believe you'll speak of them.)

12. Be prepared to discuss how much money you expect.

13. Be prepared to discuss many questions about work. Take samples.

14. Never talk about how badly you need a job.

15. Never mention personal problems of any kind.

16. Keep the interview technical, fitting, and to the point.

17. Never argue nor apologize over anything (with respect to your capabilities).

18. Ask all the questions you need to know.

19. Always thank them for their time with you.

20. Ask for the job, if you really want it. (Be firm and ask them to hire you.)

21. Always make a certain date or time to follow up with the interviewer.

## POST INTERVIEW

Following the interview, always leave a resume, photo, and calling card with phone numbers where you can be reached and a message number if you are out. A separate paragraph should probably be written about leaving phone numbers where an applicant can be reached by his family, the counselors, employers, neighbors, etc. It is of great importance that you can be contacted if something comes up with respect to your future.

Immediately after the interview, send a letter back to the person that interviewed you and include the following four main items, at least, but keep it simple. The more writing a busy person has to read, the less interested he becomes, if it's from a prospective employee. Be sincere, open and honest.

1. You appreciated her time.

2. You liked the company.

3. Ask for the job.

4. List phone numbers.

The follow-up can make the difference of an ambitious person getting a position and one who is being passed over for someone else. Again this is the salesmanship of your search. (Don't let ambition become pushy.)

Don't forget: the "thank you' letter that needs to be mailed, the visit when in the neighborhood, and

*Robert Lee Bauer*
the follow-up call to ask for the job, after four days

or more.

*Successful Job Hunting*

Interview Log:

Name: _____

Company: _____

Address: _____

_____

Telephone: _____

_____

Date/Time: _____

Directions: _____

_____

_____

Notes: _____

_____

_____

_____

_____

*Robert Lee Bauer*

Name: _____

Company: _____

Address: _____

_____

Telephone: _____

Date/Time: _____

Directions: _____

_____

_____

Notes: _____

_____

_____

_____

_____

*Successful Job Hunting*

Notes and Tasks:

<u>Places to Call</u>     <u>Phone Number</u>

*Robert Lee Bauer*

# Accepting

# CHAPTER IV
# ACCEPTING

## CONFIRMATION

The Personnel Department (Human Resources) notifying you that you have landed a great job is always good news, but don't accept too hastily. Check the conditions, actual wages, actual tasks decided, location, travel involved, contract, and all details of every concern before accepting the job.

Find out when you are to start work and where you are to report. Learn all the conditions on your acceptance. Do you have to pass a physical examination? At whose expense? When? Where?

*Robert Lee Bauer*

Do you need to submit to a credit check, background clearance check, drug testing, capability of bonding, or any other conditions?

## REVIEW

Check all aspects of the hiring conditions. When does insurance become effective, are dependents able to be covered, how about hospitalization, union dues, parking fees, course certifications, transportation expenses? Learn all the rules and regulations you will be expected to live by. Learn all that you can before accepting the job.

*Robert Lee Bauer*
## ACCEPTANCE

Accept the job by notifying the person you will be working for, and also by notifying the Personnel Department (Human Resources) and any outside agencies with whom you are working.

## SUMMARY

Remember, professional job searching is a "sales" type of task and few are capable of keeping it from affecting their outlook. You are not along. <u>It is inherent in the task</u>! Reading this book slowly and thoroughly <u>once weekly</u> can alleviate the problem and lean you <u>toward success</u>. Write notes on every page. Personalize this book completely to your needs, likes, wants and situation. Complete all lists/forms. Read it weekly cover-to-cover. <u>Gook Luck</u>!

*Robert Lee Bauer*

    Checklist for Accepting:

Start Date: _____

Title: _____

Responsibilities Include: _____

Report Directly to: _____

Wages Are: _____

Hours/Days: _____

Travel Required: _____

Wage Increase Timeline: _____

Commissions/Bonuses/Extra Monies: _____

Mileage To/From Work: _____

Gas/Expenses/Reimbursements: _____

Medical/Life Policies: _____

Licenses/Degrees/Certifications/Dues: _____

Advancement Possibilities: _____

## LIST OF ITEMS

Dates:

- 200 resumes (recommended quantity)　　_____

- 200 photos (recommended quantity)　　_____

- Quantity and date mailed　　_____

- Chamber of Commerce books checked　　_____

- Yellow Pages checked　　_____

- Newspapers/magazines/trade journals　　_____

- Friends, neighbors, family　　_____

- Put ads in papers　　_____

- Visit companies　　_____

- Visit State and County offices　　_____

- Apply for unemployment benefits　　_____

- Apply at State Employment Office　　_____

*Robert Lee Bauer*

- Review debts/savings/monies  _____

- Visit employment agencies  _____

- Check computer sites  _____

- Follow goals/plans/inventories  _____

- Review "Resume Laws" and "Interview Laws"  _____

- Review all chapters and lists  _____

- Keep a log of all places visited  _____

- Put in eight hours a day applying for jobs  _____

- Keep reviewing lists and logs  _____

*Successful Job Hunting*

# "To Do" List:

## Item                                    Date:

*Robert Lee Bauer*
"Phone Numbers" To Call:

Person/Place                                         Phone:

_____          _____

_____          _____

_____          _____

_____          _____

_____          _____

_____          _____

_____          _____

_____          _____

_____          _____

_____          _____

*Successful Job Hunting*
## NOTES – NOTES – NOTES

Item                                       Phone      Date

*Robert Lee Bauer*
## NOTES – NOTES – NOTES

*Successful Job Hunting*
NOTES – NOTES – NOTES

*Robert Lee Bauer*

# ABOUT THE AUTHOR

Robert Lee Bauer was born in Kansas City, Missouri. He is a twenty-one-year resident of the Phoenix valley in Arizona, a published author, holds a bachelors degree in business and will receive his MBA this year, en route to his Ph.D.

He has been a counselor in employment agencies and owned his own agency. He is a thirty-year member of The American Society for Quality. Now living and writing in Chandler, Arizona, he is married to a former Green Bay, Wisconsin lady and they have three grown children.

M439483

Printed in the United Kingdom
by Lightning Source UK Ltd.
109258UKS00001B/253